HOW TO IMPROVE AT
SKATEBOARDING

*All the information you need to know
to get on top of your game!*

More than just instructional guides, the **HOW TO IMPROVE AT...** *series
gives you everything you need to achieve your goals — tips on technique,
step-by-step demonstrations, nutritional advice, and the secrets of
successful pro athletes. Excellent visual instructions and expert advice
combine to act as your own personal trainer. These books aim to give
you the know-how and confidence to improve your performance.*

*Studies have shown that an active approach to life makes you feel happier
and less stressed. The easiest way to start is by taking up a new sport or
improving your skills in an existing one. You simply have to choose an
activity that enthuses you.*

HOW TO IMPROVE AT SKATEBOARDING *does not promise instant success. It
simply gives you the tools to become the best at whatever you choose to do.*

*Every care has been taken to ensure that these instructions are safe to follow, but in the
event of injury Crabtree Publishing shall not be liable for any injuries or damages.*

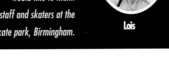

*Andrew Horsley has been designing and shooting
photos for Sidewalk skateboarding magazine
since its inception in 1995. Although Andrew is
36 years old he still enjoys skateboarding on a
regular basis. Andrew has written other books on
skateboarding including Clash Skateboarding and
Radical Sports - Skateboarding.*

Mitchell   **Herschel**

Lois   **Chris**

*ticktock Media Ltd
would like to thank
Brian Darby, staff and skaters at the
Creation skate park, Birmingham.*

Crabtree Publishing Company
www.crabtreebooks.com

Author: Andy Horsley

Editors: John Crossingham, Annabel Savery

Proofreader: Adrianna Morganelli

Project coordinator: Robert Walker

Prepress technician: Margaret Amy Salter

Production coordinator: Margaret Amy Salter

Designer: Graham Rich

Managing Editor: Rachel Tisdale

Photographer: Andrew Horsley

Planning and production by Discovery Books Ltd.

Photo credits:

Getty Images: Jeanne Rice: p. 47

Library and Archives Canada Cataloguing in Publication

Horsley, Andy
        How to improve at skateboarding / Andy Horsley.

(How to improve at--)
Includes index.
!SBN 978-0-7787-3575-5 (bound).--ISBN 978-0-7787-3597-7 (pbk.)

        1. Skateboarding--Juvenile literature. I. Title. II. Series:
How to improve at--

GV859.8.H66 2009   j796.22   C2008-907844-6

Library of Congress Cataloging-in-Publication Data

Horsley, Andy, 1972-
    How to improve at skateboarding / Andy Horsley.
        p. cm. -- (How to improve at--)
    Includes index.
    ISBN 978-0-7787-3597-7 (pbk. : alk. paper) -- ISBN 978-0-7787-3575-5
(reinforced library binding : alk. paper)
    1. Skateboarding--Juvenile literature. I. Title. II. Series.

GV859.8.H656 2009
796.22--dc22

                                        2008054542

Crabtree Publishing Company

www.crabtreebooks.com   1-800-387-7650

**Published in Canada
Crabtree Publishing**
616 Welland Ave.
St. Catharines, Ontario
L2M 5V6

**Published in the United States
Crabtree Publishing**
PMB16A
350 Fifth Ave., Suite 3308
New York, NY 10118

Published in 2009 by CRABTREE PUBLISHING COMPANY

CONTENTS

INTRODUCTION

Welcome to the fast and furious world of skateboarding. This sport is about more than just a board and four wheels. A skater's world is full of maze-like skateparks, unbelievable tricks, secret "skatespeak," and daring pros. This book is here to let you into that exciting world. You can start by learning some basics, or challenge your skills with some high-end tricks that test even the masters!

SKATESPEAK

Just getting to know skateboarding?
Here is a guide to the terms used in this book.

Coping - *The metal edge running along the top of a ramp or block.*
Fakie - *Riding backwards.*
Goofy - *Skaters who skate with the right foot forward, at the front of the deck.*
Grind - *When the trucks grind along coping or metal.*
Rail - *A metal rail found in skateparks or in public spaces. Hand rails are usually set into the center of a set of stairs or sometimes down the center of a flatbank*
Regular - *Skaters who skate with the left foot forward, at the front of the deck.*
Shred - *To skate fast and confidently.*
Transition - *The curve at a bottom of a ramp that helps you ride up the surface*

GUIDE TO ARROWS

Throughout the book we have used red arrows like this ➡ to indicate the action of the body and direction the skateboard is traveling.

EQUIPMENT

Before you start skateboarding you need a skateboard setup. A setup includes a deck, a pair of trucks and a set of wheels, plus a few other smaller parts. These important parts are all put together to make your skateboard.

SKATEBOARD DECK

A typical skateboard deck is made from seven plies, **or layers, of Canadian maple wood glued and pressed together. These plies make the deck strong but flexible.**

TAIL: Similar to the nose but at the rear of the deck. It is more rounded than the nose.

GRIPTAPE

Griptape is like sandpaper. It's stuck on top of the deck so your feet stay steady as you ride. Griptape also makes it easier to flip the board with your feet. Griptape should be applied before adding the trucks to your board.

BELLY: The section in between the nose and the tail.

CONCAVE: This is a slight dip, or valley, that runs down the middle of the deck.

TRUCKS

The trucks allow you to turn, by leaning forward or backward as you move. By tightening or loosening the nut on the kingpin, you can adjust each truck until you feel comfortable with the way the skateboard carves.

AXLE: Your wheels are bolted onto this steel rod, which runs through the hanger.

KINGPIN: The bolt that holds the hanger onto the baseplate.

BUSHINGS: Two rubber doughnuts that sit around the kingpin. They help control the steering.

HANGER: The main body of the truck. You grind on the hanger.

BASEPLATE: This piece bolts onto the deck.

NUTS AND BOLTS

A set of eight nuts and bolts hold the trucks to the deck. Most skateboarding bolts come with an Allen key included in the package.

BOLT HOLES: Four holes at the front and four at the back used to attach the trucks.

WHEELS

All skateboard wheels are made from a hard plastic called urethane. Usually they are white but colored wheels are also available. Each wheel holds a bearing in each side.

NOSE: The rounded front end of the deck. It lifts up slightly and is a bit more pointy than the tail.

BEARINGS

Bearings come in packs of eight — two for each wheel. A bearing's speed and quality is measured in an ABEC rating. ABEC 3 are basic bearings. High quality speedbearings are ABEC 7. The best bearings are ceramic, but are very expensive.

SKATE TOOL

A skatetool tightens or loosens nuts when adjusting your wheels or trucks. Keep a skatetool in your bag or pocket when out skating to easily care for loose nuts or bolts.

KNOW YOUR TERRAIN

The term skateboarding terrain can mean many places — from your own backyard to a huge ramp in a world class tournament. Some great terrain can be easily found at your local skatepark. Before you start shredding, let's take some time to learn about the obstacles you'll find there.

Indoor skatepark

TRANSITIONS

Almost all skateparks will have some form of transition.

A transition is any obstacle made from wood that has a bend or curve in it. **Quarter pipes** have one transition, or bend. They can be anywhere from two feet (60 cm) to 30 feet (ten m) high! **Mini-ramps** and **vert ramps** have two transitions facing each other. This lets you go from one transition to another without stopping. Transitions can be tight or mellow depending on the curve—the steeper the curve, the tighter the transition. Tight transitions are harder to skate. When learning to skate, make sure you start on the mellow ones!

HANDRAILS

Handrails are where the more confident skateboarders spend much of their time.

Handrails are made from steel and come in different sizes and steepness. Handrails are either placed in the center of a set of stairs or down the center of a **flatbank**. Do not try these obstacles until you have the confidence and skill to skate them. Learn to grind on a **flatbar** first and then gradually try handrails.

Handrail

Flatbank

Transition

TOP TIP
Never skate handrails or vert ramps by yourself! Always skate these obstacles with a bunch of friends. If you injure yourself, there will be help close by! Always wear pads when on handrails or vert ramps.

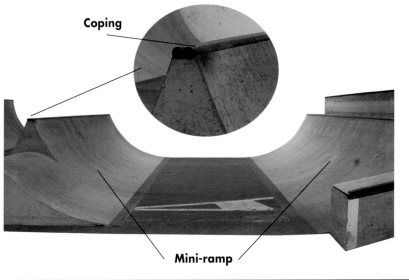

Coping

Mini-ramp

Mini-ramps are great fun and come in many sizes. Most are around four to five feet (1.2 - 1.5 m) high and about 18 feet (5.4 m) wide. *They have transitions on both sides. Skaters drop in on the ramp from the platforms on either end. Skaters try to* **carve**, **grind** *and slide for as long as possible. Each transition has a length of steel tubing running along the top called the* **coping**. *You grind and slide on the coping.*

Vert ramps are the big daddy of the mini-ramp. *Verts differ in size, but the transitions always has a 1 to 2 foot (30-60 cm) vertical section at the top. These ramps are very tall. When you drop in one side, you go so fast that you catch air on the other side. This means that you fly up above the top and then land back into the ramp. Skaters build speed moving back and forth between the two transitions. It takes a long time to perfect riding these ramps. Pads and a helmet must be worn at all times. Start by doing big long carves from the bottom, then work your way up the ramp. Always take it one step at a time.*

Vert ramp Vertical section

Blocks **of various sizes are scattered around the skatepark. Some are placed on the floor, others run down the sides of flatbanks.** *Blocks are great for learning how to slide and grind. Start on smaller blocks and work your way up. You will need to learn the ollie (page 14) in order to grind or slide these obstacles. Flatbars are lengths of freestanding steel coping placed around the park. These are great for learning how to balance your weight. Flatbars require excellent control and balance. Learn boardslides and grinds on blocks first, then try them on the flatbar.*

Block

Flatbar

WARMING UP & PADDING UP

Before you can "get gnarly" for an entire skating session, you need to get your muscles stretched and warmed up. Even after you've done these simple stretches, always start your session slowly. Do some basic maneuvers on the ground, then you can hit the ramps, bars, and blocks.

This stretch gets you ready for the next few stretches.
Sit down with both legs together. Support one leg with your hand and slowly slide the foot of the other leg up to your knee. Switch legs and repeat.

Use the same position as the first stretch.
Place the opposite hand on the inside of your bent knee. At the same time swing the other arm behind you so that it lines up with the straight leg. Push down on the bent knee and swing your shoulders and hips around so that you stretch your back muscles. Repeat on the other side.

After you've stretched your knee a few times, try touching your toes.
Sit down with your legs flat against the floor. Keep your back as straight as you can and touch both sets of toes. This stretches the shoulder, back and arm muscles you use when you are reaching for your deck during a grab.

Skateboarding is hard on your Achilles tendon (this is the big tendon that connects your heel to the back of your leg)
Stand on tip toes with your heels hanging off the edge of a small curb. Your heels should be in mid-air. Keep your feet as firm as possible and slowly lean forward so that you can feel the back of your heels gently stretching. Do this for around a minute.

Finish with a simple knee stretch.
Stand upright and lift one foot up behind you so that you are standing on one leg. Grab your foot and gently pull to stretch your knee muscles. Repeat with the other leg.

TOP TIP
Have a quick jog on the spot and shake your arms to get the blood flowing.

Most skateboard parks require you to wear pads and a helmet. This is a good thing to do, especially if you are still learning. Elbows and knees are often the first body parts to hit the floor if you take a slam. All good skateparks will have a set of pads that you can either borrow or rent. Even the pros wear pads, so get padded up!

HELMET

The skateboard helmet is made from tough plastics and is lined with a comfortable foam layer.

You can get custom helmets designed with your favorite skateboard company's logos. There are thousands of different designs, so it's easy to grab yourself a unique skid lid!

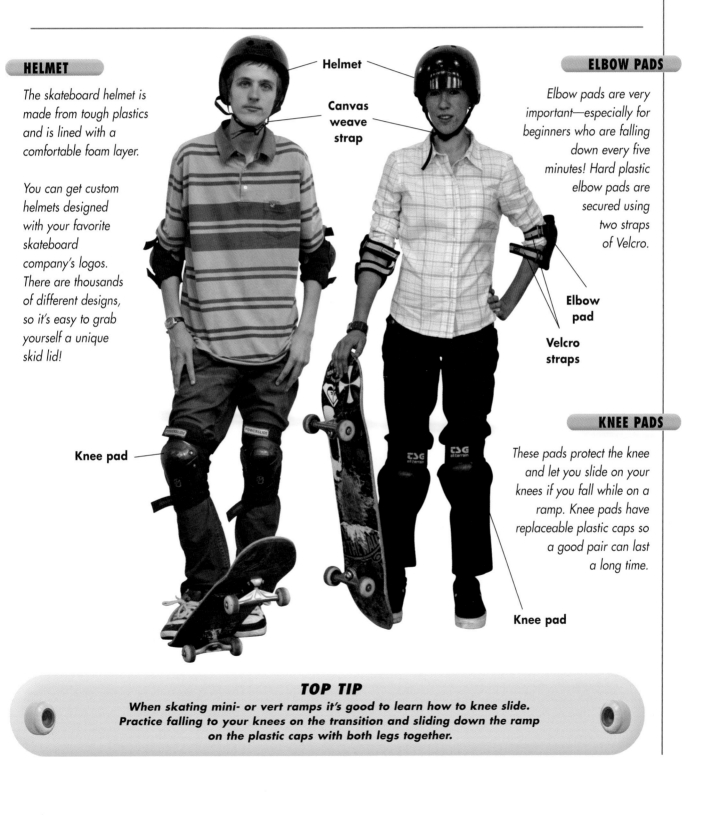

Helmet

Canvas weave strap

Knee pad

ELBOW PADS

Elbow pads are very important—especially for beginners who are falling down every five minutes! Hard plastic elbow pads are secured using two straps of Velcro.

Elbow pad

Velcro straps

KNEE PADS

These pads protect the knee and let you slide on your knees if you fall while on a ramp. Knee pads have replaceable plastic caps so a good pair can last a long time.

Knee pad

TOP TIP

When skating mini- or vert ramps it's good to learn how to knee slide. Practice falling to your knees on the transition and sliding down the ramp on the plastic caps with both legs together.

PUSHING OFF

Now that you are warmed up and ready to rock, it's time get moving on all four wheels. This is called "pushing off." The more confident that you are pushing off, the quicker and more fluid you will be. Before you can perform a good push, you need to see if you are regular or goofy stance...

Whether you are regular or goofy depends on which foot feels most natural at the front of the deck. By the way, goofy doesn't mean stupid and regular doesn't mean normal! These are just terms that were made up by surfers long before skateboarding. Just think of it as being "left handed" or "right handed."

REGULAR FOOT

This is when you skate with your left foot forward (at the front of the deck).

GOOFY FOOT

This is when you skate with your right foot forward (at the front of the deck).

Begin pushing off with your leading foot at the front of the deck. Place your toes somewhere around the front truck bolts. This helps you keep the deck balanced on all four wheels. Now push off with your back foot away from the floor. This propels the board forwards. The harder and farther you stretch your leg as you push, the faster you will go. Goofy footers push on the left hand side of the deck, while regular is on the right hand side.

TOP TIP

To discover your stance, find a smooth floor surface. Run and slide in your socks. Which foot do you naturally put in front? Place this foot at the front of your skateboard stance.

Once you have pushed off with a few solid strokes, you then plant your pushing foot onto the deck.
Place your back foot over the rear truck bolts—you can see the bolt heads on top of your griptape. When you are stable and rolling confidently, you will need to slowly turn your front foot from pointing forward to sideways. Now your stance is perfectly balanced for carving, turning and tricks.

STEP 1
Start from a standstill. Place your leading foot on the front of the deck and your pushing foot on the ground next to the back wheel.

You should keep your balance and body weight over the center of the skateboard.

STEP 2
Leaning on your front foot, slowly start to push forward with your pushing leg.

As you push, your foot will naturally start to shift to your toes.

STEP 3
As you finish pushing, your foot will come off the ground. Keeping your weight over the center of the skateboard, start to bring your pushing leg on the deck.

STEP 4
As the board rolls forward, place your pushing foot on the back of the deck. In order to keep your balance, your back foot should rest over the rear truck bolts.

MOVING, TURNING & CARVING

Now you're moving! Once you can push off and stay balanced, it's time to explore all the turns, carves and tricks of skateboarding. The easiest and first thing to learn is turning the board while riding forward.

FOOT POSITION

This picture shows your stance while you are moving forward.
Your feet should be over both sets of truck bolts and centered across the deck. Both your heels and toes will hang off the deck.

HEELSIDE PRESSURE

Press down on to the heelside of the skateboard while moving forward.
*As you apply pressure, you'll slowly but surely begin to turn. This heel-based turn is called a **frontside** carve because you turn with your chest facing out to the front side. The harder you lean, the faster and tighter the turn.*

**Apply pressure
with heel.**

TOESIDE PRESSURE

**Now press down toward the toeside
of the deck as you move.**
*This move starts a **backside** carve. As you
put pressure on the deck with your toes,
you turn with your back facing outward
from the carve.*

**Apply pressure
with toes.**

FRONTSIDE CARVE

STEP 1

Reach a comfortable speed and put pressure on the heelside of the deck. Move your arms out to keep your body balanced.

STEP 2

The skateboard should turn to the side. Keep applying pressure and stay balanced as you turn.

STEP 3

To stop carving, release the pressure and your board will straighten out again. You can do these turns as slowly or as quickly as you want.

BACKSIDE CARVE

STEP 1

Reach a comfortable speed and put pressure on the deck with your toes. You will feel the skateboard starting to turn. Hold out your arms to stay balanced if you need to.

STEP 2

The pressure from your toes will have you carving backside. Lean back a little with your upper body to stay balanced.

STEP 3

At the end of the carve, release the pressure from your toes and you will straighten out. These turns are great for carving around a long bend.

TOP TIP

As you become more at home with these carves, try changing smoothly from one to another. This creates a winding snake effect. Push away a few times and then do as many backside to frontside carves as you can!

THE OLLIE

The ollie is THE most important trick you will ever learn on a skateboard. Not only is it a pretty cool trick on its own, nearly every other skating trick uses an ollie.

THE OLLIE

The ollie is the skateboard jump. When you've learned this trick, you'll be able to hop up onto objects and leap over things. These four steps happen very quickly — in the blink of an eye!

STEP 1

Put your front foot just behind the four front truck bolts. Take up the correct foot position for the ollie. Crouch down slightly with your knees bent.

Bend knees

Your back foot should be at the very back of the deck with your toes in the middle of the tail.

Correct foot positioning for the ollie.

Put your front foot just behind the four front truck bolts

STEP 2

Kick down on the tail with your back foot as hard as you can. You'll hear a "POP" as it smacks the floor. As you kick down, come off your front leg to let the board's nose point upward.

STEP 3

Now you need to jump. At the same time, scrape the side of your front foot along the griptape and lift your back foot. This is an ollie scrape. Your front foot drags the board into the air and the release of the back leg allows the board to come up.

Slide front foot up griptape.

Release pressure from back foot.

STEP 4

Keep your balance over the deck. Follow your skateboard back to the ground. As you hit the ground with all four wheels at the same time, crouch a little to stay balanced. You've just popped an ollie!

THE OLLIE WHILE MOVING

Now try the ollie while moving forward. This movement helps with the fluid motion you need to pop a really good ollie.

STEP 1

Push off and keep your body weight over the deck. Crouch down slightly.

STEP 2

As your speed evens out, get ready to kick down on the tail with your back foot.

STEP 3

Kick down hard and lift the pressure off the front foot. Then drag your front foot sideways up the griptape and release the pressure from your back leg. Your board should level out in the air.

STEP 4

Bring your board back to the ground and keep your balance over the deck. When you hit the ground, bend your knees slightly as you land. Continue skating away. The trick to learning the ollie is to never give up. It may take a while, but once you learn it you'll know it forever!

Bend your knees slightly when you land.

HOW TO FLIP THE BOARD

Most skateboarders can't wait to try flipping their board but it's a tricky trick to learn! Flips take a lot of practice to perfect and before you can flip the board, you must master how to ollie first. After that, the kickflip is probably the first flip trick you will successfully learn. So follow these steps and get flipping!

HOW TO FLIP THE BOARD

This trick begins with an ollie. The back foot stays in the normal ollie position (toes in the center of the tail), but the front foot is placed slightly off the deck **toward the** heel edge.

Front foot

Back foot

Correct foot positions for a flip.

STEP 1

Start moving at a medium speed. Hit down on the tail with some force, jump and start to scrape your front foot up the griptape.

STEP 2

As you scrape your front foot up the tape, start to scrape it toward the heel edge of the deck (in a normal ollie you only scrape forward). This motion starts the deck turning. Remember to stay central over the deck at all times.

TOP TIP

Try learning this trick standing still or even on a carpeted surface. Some people find it helpful to practice on a deck with no wheels or trucks. If you can perfect this foot flick, you're on your way to mastering the kickflip!

STEP 3

This part is called the flick. As your front foot scrapes up and off edge of the deck, it flicks the board around. The scrape must be done quickly to flick the board.

Now the deck is in full motion and should be turning underneath your body and feet.

STEP 4

Watch the board turn underneath you. As the deck turns a full 360° along its length the griptape side of the board becomes visible.

Once the tape appears, get your feet ready to step over the truck bolts for landing.

STEP 5

As your feet "catch" the board get ready to ride away at the same speed as before the trick. The kickflip is about trial and error—practice is the key. This awesome trick is a must for any skater so keep at it!

TOP TIP
Always stay above the board as it goes through the kickflip motion.
Keep your shoulders above your feet throughout the trick.

HOW TO MAKE IT GRIND

Another type of trick that goes great with a good ollie is the grind. There are many styles of grind—the easiest one is the 50-50 grind. This is where both trucks grind along a surface at the same time. The 50-50 can be done on ledges, handrails, bars, coping at the top of ramps, and on blocks.

MAKE IT GRIND

To perform a 50-50 grind, you need to start with an ollie slightly higher than the surface that you want to grind. Go slightly faster than usual. You will need that extra speed to keep moving as your trucks grind across the surface.

STEP 1

As you approach the block hit the tail and start your ollie about one foot (30 cm) away from the obstacle. You are aiming to get both of your trucks onto the lip of the obstacle.

STEP 2

After you've ollied high enough to get onto the block, level out the deck and trucks over the grinding edge. Aim to hit the block with the middle of both trucks. Your body weight needs to be centered over the board.

Stand over the truck bolts and keep your body weight over the moving board.

STEP 3

As you land you will feel some resistance. This is the truck's metal dragging over the metal grinding edge. The faster you are traveling before you ollie, the easier it is to keep grinding. If you stop dead, try go faster next time. You can also lean back slightly as you grind.

STEP 4

At the end of your grind, lift the front of the deck upward slightly to help you drop off the edge. Simply apply weight to the tail and lift up the nose. This move lets you land with all four wheels rather than dipping down or falling backward.

STEP 5

As you end the grind, make sure all four wheels land on the floor. You should be moving fast enough to ride away smoothly.

Correct position of trucks when grinding.

TOP TIP

Never try to grind an edge that hasn't been waxed first. Simply apply a thin layer of skate wax along the surface. This reduces resistance and helps you grind smoothly. You can also apply wax directly to your trucks.

SLIDING A FLATBAR

*T*he 50-50 grind helps you develop your balance as a skater. Now it's time to try the ultimate balance trick—the boardslide on a freestanding flatbar. This trick is performed down handrails. It is often the first trick a pro does to test out a handrail that goes down stairs.

SLIDING A FLATBAR

STEP 1

This is called a backside boardslide. Roll toward the bar with your heels and back facing the bar. You will slide quite fast with this trick. Practice often to get comfortable at faster speeds.

STEP 2

Use a frontside ollie to land sideways onto the bar. You need to perform half a frontside ollie to do this.

Pop the tail on the floor and start your ollie.

STEP 3

As you ollie, throw your shoulders around slightly so that the momentum takes you onto the bar.

STEP 4

Get ready to balance as you center the board on the bar. You will start to slide along. By now you will be facing frontward as you slide.

It's very important to keep the deck level and your weight balanced across the board.

STEP 5

Hold this pose until you near the end of the bar. Get ready to turn the board forward as you come off. If you don't turn, you will come to a nasty stop!

STEP 6

At the end of the boardslide, start turning the deck forward to ride away. Don't do this until the board can come off the bar cleanly.

Use your front leg to push the front of the deck away from the bar.

STEP 7

The skateboard should now be clear of the bar. Keep turning the deck around until you are skating in the same direction you were before the trick. Nice one!

TOP TIP

When in the middle of the boardslide, your chest should be facing the way that you are sliding. Use your arms to keep you level on the bar. Imagine that you are walking on a tightrope!

DROPPING IN ON A RAMP

Skating on flat ground makes it easy to control your speed and direction. Once you're ready for a new challenge, it's time to drop in and skate some transitions.

TRANSITIONS

A transition is a bend or curve in a ramp. Basically anything with a curve in can be called a transition. A big vert ramp has two transitions, one at each side. It's easier to practice dropping in on a quarterpipe first. These have only one transition and lead out onto the flat ground instead of another transition.

DROPPING IN

Start by placing your deck on the transition by hand at first. Climb up onto the ramp and place the tail on the coping on edge of the ramp.

STEP 1

Hold the tail firmly against the coping with your back foot. Check that everything is locked solid. Rest your front foot on the side until you're ready.

STEP 2

Move your front foot from the platform of the ramp onto the truck bolts near the nose. Keep your weight on your back foot for now.

Hold the tail of the board against the metal coping.

Coping

Move your front foot onto the nose of the board.

The key to dropping in well is confidence. As long as you are well-padded during this trick you will be fine.

Hold your arms out to steady yourself.

Bend your knees

STEP 3

When you have both feet on the deck start to lean forward. You will start moving very fast so keep your feet on the griptape at all times.

STEP 4

As you start to drop into the transition, lean forward and get ready for some speed! Stamp down on your front wheels as soon as you leave the coping. This gets all four wheels down as early as possible. Stay with the board as it rides down the ramp.

TOP TIP

Stamp the board down so that it follows the transition of the ramp and doesn't do a wheelie all the way to the floor.

ROCK & ROLL

*T*he *"Rock & Roll" is a traditional trick often used when skating a ramp. In this trick, you ride up the transition rather than down it. Skaters drop in on one side and then do a rock & roll up the other side. Now you know how to drop in, maybe it's time for some rock and roll!*

ROCK & ROLL

STEP 1

Ride toward the transition with enough speed to reach the coping. Keep both your feet stable over the truck bolts. Bend your knees slightly and stay relaxed as you hit the ramp.

Bend knees

Coping

STEP 2

Keeping the same body position, start to ride up the transition. Get ready to hit the coping at the top of the ramp. Look at the coping and picture the center of your board balancing on it.

STEP 3

At the top of the ramp, lift the front wheels slightly as you go past the coping. Just don't go too far! Stay with your board as it reaches the top.

STEP 4

As the center of your board reaches the coping, push down with your front foot. Balance the board's belly on the coping.

Belly of the board makes contact with the coping.

STEP 5

As soon as you feel contact between the board and the coping, it's time to turn back down into the ramp.

STEP 6

With the "Rock" completed it's time for the "Roll." As you come away from the coping, put pressure on the tail and swing the nose back around away from the ramp.

Lift the nose by putting pressure on the tail.

STEP 7

The turn in a rock & roll comes from your shoulders. Swing your arms around to help turn the board.

Swing the board around on the back wheels.

STEP 8

Put the front wheels down so that you ride off on all four. The rock & roll is a quick trick. Begin by learning it in sections. Practice dropping in and riding up and down transitions to build your confidence.

ROCK FAKIE

The rock fakie is the dangerous brother of the rock & roll. This trick also involves riding up the transition and lapping over the coping. This time, you ride back in fakie! It's easy to get stuck on the coping during this trick. Confidence will help you master this trick.

HOW TO ROCK FAKIE

Like other transition tricks, keep your feet solid over the truck bolts and try not to shuffle about on the deck too much.

Top edge

Bend knees

STEP 1

Approach the transition and keep your eyes on the top edge. As you start to enter the ramp bend your knees slightly. This will keep you relaxed and well balanced.

STEP 2

As you near the coping, begin to press down on the tail with your back foot. This lifts the nose so that you lap over the coping.

Pressing down on the tail will lift the nose.

STEP 3

Once your front wheels are past the coping and the center of the deck is in line with the edge, settle the board down.

Center of the deck

STEP 4
Your board should now be balanced on the edge of the coping, as in a boardslide .

STEP 5
Now you need to go back down the transition fakie.

Gravity will take you back down the ramp. Lift the front wheels to unlock the board from the coping.

STEP 6
This happens quickly so be prepared! Keep your body balanced over the board as you ride down the transition.

STEP 7
Wipe the sweat from your brow as you ride away fakie.

BACKSIDE 50-50 AXLE STALLS

After you master dropping in, rock & rolls, and rock fakies, the next step is to get your trucks on the coping. Once you learn this 50-50 axle stall, you will have all sorts of different tricks to help you skate ramps with ease.

THE 50-50 AXLE STALL

Coping

STEP 1

Ride up toward the coping. You need enough speed to get the whole board up on the top of the ramp.

STEP 2

As you reach the coping lift your front wheels slightly to let them pass the edge. You are aiming to lap your back truck onto the coping.

Lift front wheels.

Press down on the tail to lift front wheels.

STEP 3

As you feel the back truck touch the coping, use your legs and shoulders to turn the board. The nose should swing around and be parallel with the coping.

TOP TIP

The 50-50 axle stall is a blind trick because you can't see the trucks touch the coping. As your back trucks lap over the coping, you will feel a slight thud—this is when you know it's safe to put the front trucks down too. Practice until you can "feel" this trick with your feet.

STEP 4

When the front trucks are over the coping, set them down. You should now be standing over the skateboard with both trucks firmly on the coping.

Correct position for trucks.

STEP 5

Time to escape! As soon as you have balanced on both trucks, lift the front truck again and get ready to turn back into the transition.

STEP 6

Swing the front of the deck back down into the transition. Treat the next stage just like dropping in (see pages 22-23), except you leave from the truck rather than the tail.

STEP 7

Gravity does the rest. Trust your board and stay balanced as you ride away.

FRONTSIDE & BACKSIDE OLLIE

There are hundreds of tricks that can be done on a skateboard. After you've learned the basic ones, you can start combining tricks together—you can even make up your own! These next pages are full of complex tricks to help you become master of the skatepark.

FRONTSIDE 180 OLLIE

The frontside 180 ollie is where your chest is thrown forward to turn you 180°.

STEP 1
This is an ollie with a 180° turn in mid-air. First, get your feet in a normal ollie position.

STEP 2
Hit the tail. Swing your arms for extra momentum.

STEP 3
As you do the ollie scrape, throw your body around 90° and take your board with it.

STEP 4
By now, your deck should have moved around 180° in the air.

STEP 5
When the skateboard has turned a full 180° put the front wheels down first. Then settle the back wheels down and ride away fakie.

STEP 1

This is the opposite of a frontside ollie—you throw your body around toward your back this time. Get your feet in the ollie position.

The backside ollie is where your back is thrown round to turn you 180°.

STEP 3

After you are in the air throw your body and board around 90°.

STEP 2

Hit the tail, do an ollie scrape and swing your arms and hips into a backside movement.

STEP 4

You can turn this trick 90° before you hit the floor—you will need to slide the other 90°.

STEP 5

As you touch down slide the board around until you are riding away fakie.

FRONTSIDE & BACKSIDE FLIPS

We are going to start mixing tricks together. The frontside flip is a frontside ollie and a kickflip combined. The same goes for the backside flip. Both tricks are crowd pleasers and can be done down stairs or across gaps. Instead of just ollieing on to something, add a flip and impress your friends.

THE FRONTSIDE FLIP

STEP 1

This trick begins just like a frontside 180° ollie except you hang your front foot slightly off the heel edge as with the kickflip.

STEP 2

Scrape and kick out to the side. As you ollie 90°, get ready to flick at the same time.

STEP 3

By the middle of the kickflip, you need to frontside ollie the board and kick out to the side.

STEP 4

The board flips and turns 180°. Stay above it at all times. When the board's four wheels are down, ride away fakie.

STEP 1
This time, you will throw the board around 180° with your back facing forward. As you're about to hit the tail start your body swinging around backside.

STEP 2
Pop the tail and start a backside ollie. At the same time, get ready to kick out and to the side.

STEP 3
Once in the air, kick the board to start the flip.

STEP 4
Keep the deck under your body as you get ready to land.

STEP 5
Land with all four wheels down and ride away fakie.

THE POP SHOVE-IT & 360 KICKFLIP

*B*oth of these tricks involve turning the board around underneath you. The 360 flip is very tricky because the board turns a full circle as well as being flipped! The pop shove-it is a lot easier— you need to learn this trick in order to do a 360 flip.

THE POP SHOVE-IT

This trick helps you get used to moving the board around under your feet.

STEP 1
This trick gets its power from your back foot. Ollie, but instead of just hitting the tail, scoop it around at the same time. This starts turning the board around.

Hit the tail and scoop it around at the same time.

STEP 2
Don't scrape as much with your front foot. Just pop and scoop the board around 180° with the back foot.

STEP 3
As it comes around 180°, stay over the deck and stamp it down. Your board will now be backward under your feet.

STEP 4
Plant both feet over the truck bolts and you're ready for a clean ride away!

THE 360 KICKFLIP

With this trick, the deck is pushed around 360 while doing a kickflip. An ollie is used to get the board in the air.

STEP 1

*Place your front foot in a kickflip position with your heel off the edge of the deck. Your back foot is at the **toe edge** corner of the tail.*

Hit down and push the board around with the back foot.

Use the front foot to flip the board.

STEP 2

Begin an ollie, then start to push the board around with your back foot. At the same time, kick out to the side to do a kickflip.

STEP 3

Shove hard with your back foot to turn the board around 360°. The board should also be flipping.

STEP 4

Stay above the deck. Once it's turned 360°, be ready to land.

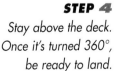

STEP 5

Stomp your feet down over the truck bolts as you land. You've just nailed one of the hardest tricks around — a 360 flip!

FRONTSIDE BOARDSLIDE & K-GRIND

The frontside boardslide is a difficult cousin of the regular boardslide (page 20-21). The K-Grind, or "krooked" grind, is a cool trick that grinds on the front truck. Both tricks are used often by pros to ride handrails but don't worry — you can easily learn them on smaller skatepark obstacles.

FRONTSIDE BOARDSLIDE

STEP 1

Face the rail with your chest. Ollie high enough to get above it. Keep your eyes on the rail.

STEP 2

As you ollie, move the deck toward the rail with your feet. You need to get the belly of the board right over it.

STEP 3

Land with the center of the deck on the flatbar and twist your body to balance over it.

STEP 4

As you slide along be aware that the end will be coming, prepare to turn off to ride away forward.

STEP 5

As you drop off the rail use your front foot to direct the board so that you ride away straight.

TOP TIP

Keep your body twisted to help stay balanced throughout the slide.

THE K-GRIND

STEP 1
Ride alongside of the box as close as you can with your back facing it.

STEP 2
Pop an ollie and use your front foot to aim the board. Jab the nose and front truck onto the edge of the box.

STEP 3
When the front truck makes contact with the box, take the weight off your back leg. This allows the back of the skateboard to rise.

STEP 4
As you reach the end of the block, push forward with your front foot. Bring your back foot down to level the board.

Correct truck position during the K-Grind.

STEP 5
Land on all four wheels. Straighten out and ride away.

Toeside wheel running freely.

The heelside of the board crushed against the inside wheel.

TOP TIP
Keep your weight forward and over the nose while doing a K-Grind. Hold out your arms to keep balanced.

SLIDE 180 & THE FAKIE KICKFLIP

There are a few different ways to ride backward, or fakie. For example, you'll end up riding fakie after a 180 ollie. Sliding around is an even easier option to head backward. You can even do a 180 slide without losing your speed. It's a perfect move to get set up for a fakie trick, such as the fakie kickflip.

STEP 1

Ride along forward with your front foot over the nose and your back foot over the tail.

SLIDE 180

STEP 2

When you are ready, give your shoulders a big swing as if you were going to spin around on the spot.

STEP 3

Use this momentum to push the rear of the deck around with your back foot.

STEP 4

As you push the deck around, pivot on the front wheels. Lift the rear wheels slightly if they are sticking.

STEP 5

Stop pushing just before you've turned around fully. Straighten up and continue riding in the same direction—only now facing backward!

STEP 1

This trick is a kickflip while riding backward. Either start off riding fakie, or use a 180 slide to turn around.

STEP 2

Get your feet in the kickflip position (see pages 16-17). Pop the ollie and flick out to the side.

STEP 3

Stay over the board as it spins.

STEP 4

As the board flips around to the griptape side, place your feet back onto the deck.

STEP 5

Land with your feet over the truckbolts and ride away fakie.

TOP TIP

Always look down at the board when trying the fakie kickflip. This trick becomes easier the more that you ride around backward, so practice!

PUMPING A VERT RAMP

Most big skateparks have a vert ramp. This ramp can look huge and scary to a beginner and it takes a while to master skating vert. Once you learn though, it can be great fun—it's like flying! Before you drop in and catch some air, it's a good idea to have a "pump around." This means taking big sweeps across the ramp from side to side, up and down, forward and fakie.

PUMPING UP THE RAMP

STEP 1

Start this move on the flat section of the vert ramp. Do a few pushes so you are traveling toward the transition.

STEP 2

When you reach the middle of the transition start to bend your legs and crouch down into the ramp. Swing your arms forward to propel you up.

Bend your knees

STEP 3

Keep your legs bent and get as high up past the transition as you feel comfortable.

STEP 4

As you slow down, you will start to come down the ramp fakie.

Start to straighten your legs.

STEP 5

Straighten up as you come back down to the flat section of the ramp. You've just pumped!

STEP 1
Ride toward the vert's transition. Start to lean in with your chest as you hit the transition, but keep your speed.

STEP 2
As you ride higher up the transition, lean farther into the ramp with your chest.

STEP 3
This leaning pushes you around so that you are horizontal with the ground. When you have reached the highest point carve down into the ramp and point the board back toward the bottom.

STEP 4
You will now start to ride forward down into the transition.

STEP 5
As you hit the transition straighten out your legs.

Now try another carve on the other wall of the ramp.

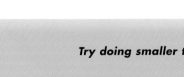

TOP TIP
**Try doing smaller tighter carves as well as big long mellow ones.
Both feel amazing!**

SKATEPARK DIET

*S*kateboarding takes loads of energy. If you want to do tricks all day, you need to have a healthy, balanced diet! Some indoor skateparks have a cafe onsite where you can get good wholesome snacks, such as baked potatoes and pasta dishes. Many skaters just pack themselves a lunch to take to the park—it's a lot cheaper.

This is the recommended intake for a balanced and healthy diet, which is essential for skateboarders.

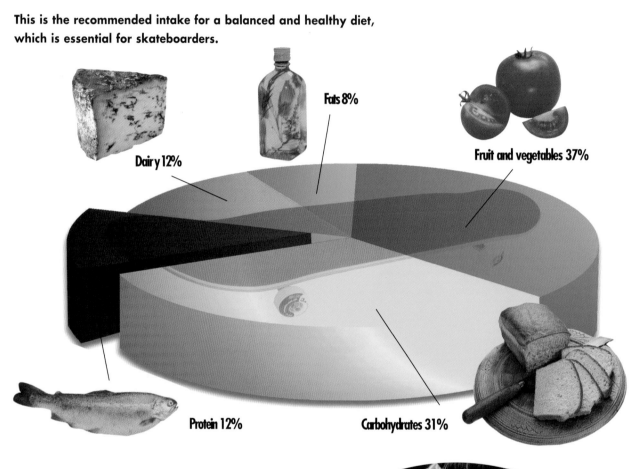

Dairy 12%

Fats 8%

Fruit and vegetables 37%

Protein 12%

Carbohydrates 31%

ENERGY BOOSTERS

Carbohydrates are great for producing energy. If you are planning a hard day's skating, make a big bowl of pasta to take along in your backpack. It's also a good idea to take some fruit as a healthy snack for later.

Most skateboarders use a lot of items to get through a fun day at the skatepark.

It's most important to keep hydrated with plenty of water, so keep a large bottle with you at all times.

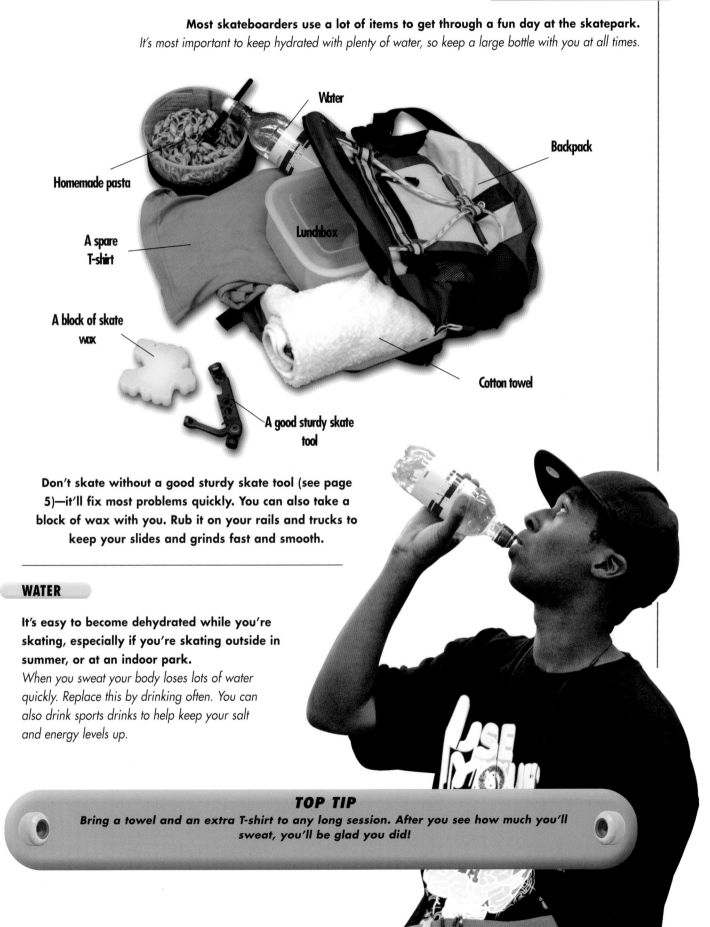

Water

Backpack

Homemade pasta

Lunchbox

A spare T-shirt

A block of skate wax

Cotton towel

A good sturdy skate tool

Don't skate without a good sturdy skate tool (see page 5)—it'll fix most problems quickly. You can also take a block of wax with you. Rub it on your rails and trucks to keep your slides and grinds fast and smooth.

WATER

It's easy to become dehydrated while you're skating, especially if you're skating outside in summer, or at an indoor park.

When you sweat your body loses lots of water quickly. Replace this by drinking often. You can also drink sports drinks to help keep your salt and energy levels up.

TOP TIP
Bring a towel and an extra T-shirt to any long session. After you see how much you'll sweat, you'll be glad you did!

INJURIES

U nfortunately, skating can lead to injuries, so wear proper protection. Common injuries are to the wrists and ankles.

WRIST

If you slam your hand down too hard you could sprain your wrist.

To help avoid a sprain when falling, roll to the side and land on your bottom. You can also buy wrist guards that have a plastic shield covering your wrist and palm. These can help prevent sprains. Never skate while you're injured—it can make things much worse!

ANKLE

Ankle injuries are also common among skateboarders.

If you twist or sprain your ankle, get ice on your ankle as soon as you can. Elevate your leg, rest, and keep your weight off it as much as possible. See your doctor to be sure it's not a serious injury. There are many ankle supports available. These help protect your ankle from injury while you skate.

**If you twist your ankle there are
a few things that you can do.**
*Put ice on there as soon as you can to help the swelling go down.
There are also a few creams and gels that can speed up
the recovery of your sprained ankle.*

ARNICA CREAM:
This is a natural product that helps bring the bruising out.
*Rub the Arnica cream on your ankle a few times a day. You
should see the bruising appear a lot faster than normal. This
helps the body disperse the bruise and get you up and skating
as soon as possible.*

TIGER BALM:
**Tiger balm is great for when you've pulled
a muscle or have sore joints.**
*This balm has a strong medical smell and warms up
the affected area. It not only brings relief and comfort
quickly, it relaxes the muscles and helps the sprain heal.*

TOP TIP
*Always skate with a group of friends. That way, if you do hurt yourself you will have
immediate help. If you do sprain a joint, do not continue skateboarding. Take time out
and rest yourself. You can always skate another day...*

HOW THE FAMOUS DO IT

*A*ll skateboarders skate for fun, but a few lucky people can make it their full-time job. Can you imagine earning money doing something that you would do for free? That's real life for pros like Tony Hawk and Geoff Rowley! Through hard work, skill and determination, they have made a pastime into a career.

GEOFF ROWLEY

Geoff Rowley started skateboarding on the streets of Liverpool, England at the age of 13.
He quickly became noticed by the British skateboard team "Deathbox" who sponsored him and took him to competitions all over Europe. Deathbox became "Flip Skateboards" and moved to the U.S.A., taking Geoff with them. Geoff soon got noticed and appeared in many U.S. skate videos and magazines. Geoff has been a professional skateboarder for over a decade and is widely thought of as the best street skater in the world. He appears on "Tony Hawk's Pro Skater" game and continues to push street skating to the limit.

Geoff Rowley lipslides a kinked handrail in his new hometown of Orange County, California.

Tony Hawk showing off his signature moves for the crowd in Orange, California.

TONY HAWK

Tony Hawk is the most famous skateboarder in the world.
He has been skateboarding for over 30 years and is probably the best vert ramp skateboarder the world has ever seen. Tony invented a lot of the vert ramp tricks that you see on TV today and in 1999 landed the first ever 900—that's two and a half spins in the air. Tony Hawk retired from competitive skateboarding when he reached 31, but still continues to skate, learn tricks and do demos. Tony has a rollercoaster ride named after him and has set up a charity named "The Tony Hawk Foundation" which helps to build skateparks in poor neighborhoods.

RISE UP THE RANKS

Becoming a pro should never be the only reason that you start skating.
If you are talented enough and do well in skateboarding competitions, pro sponsorship will come to you. Until then, just enjoy being on your board!

PROGRESSION OF A PRO SKATER

1. *Start skateboarding with your friends. Travel around your neighborhood exploring the local terrain.*
2. *Enter local competitions. If you do well maybe the local skatestore will give you a deck or a T-shirt.*
3. *If you feel you are good enough, film some tricks and send the video to your favorite skateboard company.*
4. *At this point you may start to receive monthly packages of decks, tees and wheels, etc.*
5. *Hopefully you will be entering competitions and doing well, maybe filming sections for a team video.*
6. *A small number of really good skateboarders will get their own signature shoe—and this means big money!*
7. *Travel around the world skateboarding and doing demos, and shooting photos for major skate magazines.*
8. *At the top of the pro tour you may appear in video games and TV ads.*

TOP TIP
If you think that you are good enough to be sponsored, try to enter lots of competitions and skate at the most popular skateparks. This is the best way to get noticed. There's no need to be too pushy or to show off—just enjoy skateboarding!

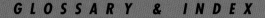

GLOSSARY

BACKSIDE — *This is either where your back is facing the obstacle that you are skating or the direction that you are carving*

BLOCK — *A flat rectangular shaped obstacle with coping on the topside edges*

CARVING — *This is where you use a ramp's transition to help you turn or "carve"*

COPING — *The metal edge running along the top of a ramp or block*

FAKIE — *Riding backwards*

FLATBANK — *A ramp without a transition or curve to it*

FLATBAR — *A free-standing length of steel*

FRONTSIDE — *This is either where your chest is facing the obstacle that you are skating or the direction that you are carving*

GOOFY — *Skaters who ride with their right foot forward at the front of the deck*

GRIND — *When the trucks drag along metal or coping*

HEEL EDGE — *The edge of your deck nearest to your heel*

MINI-RAMP — *A small ramp with transitions on both sides*

QUARTER PIPE — *This is a ramp with one transition. It stands by itself in a skatepark*

RAIL — *A raised metal bar found in skateparks or in public spaces*

REGULAR — *Skaters who skate with the left foot forward at the front of the deck*

SHRED — *To skate fast and with confidence*

TERRAIN — *This is any object or place that you skate—skateparks or ramp are kinds of terrain*

TOE EDGE — *The edge of your deck nearest to your toes*

TRANSITION — *The curve on a ramp. It helps you ride up the surface of the ramp*

VERT RAMP — *A large ramp with vertical walls above the transitions*

INDEX

Printed in the U.S.A. — CC